0.9 WBL X
0.5 pTS.

Community Helpers

Reporters

by Rebecca Pettiford

Bullfrog Books

Ideas for Parents and Teachers

Bullfrog Books let children practice reading informational text at the earliest reading levels. Repetition, familiar words, and photo labels support early readers.

Before Reading

• Discuss the cover photo. Who might this book be about?

• Look at the picture glossary together. Read and discuss the words.

Read the Book

• "Walk" through the book and look at the photos. Let the child ask questions. Point out the photo labels.

• Read the book to the child, or have him or her read independently.

After Reading

• Prompt the child to think more. Ask: Have you seen or heard a reporter at work? Where did you see him or her?

Bullfrog Books are published by Jump!
5357 Penn Avenue South
Minneapolis, MN 55419
www.jumplibrary.com

Library of Congress Cataloging-in-Publication Data

Pettiford, Rebecca.
  Reporters / by Rebecca Pettiford.
    pages cm. — (Community helpers)
  Includes index.
  ISBN 978-1-62031-159-2 (hardcover) —
  ISBN 978-1-62496-246-2 (ebook)
  1. Reporters and reporting—Juvenile literature.
  2. Journalism—Juvenile literature. I. Title.
  PN4781.P47 2015
  070.4'3—dc23
                                    2014032135

Series Editor: Wendy Dieker
Series Designer: Ellen Huber
Book Designer: Anna Peterson
Photo Researcher: Jenny Fretland VanVoorst

Photo Credits: All photos by Shutterstock except: Dreamstime, 22, 23bl; Getty, 6–7, 21; Superstock, 4; Thinkstock, 1, 13, 17, 19, 23tr.

Printed in the United States of America at Corporate Graphics in North Mankato, Minnesota.

Table of Contents

Reporters at Work

Deb wants to be a reporter.

What do they do?

What do they do?

They bring us the news.
They tell us what's
going on.

Gia is at a fair.

She has a microphone.

It helps us hear
her talk.

microphone

Oh no! A house is on fire!

The fire is out.

Ann talks to
a firefighter.

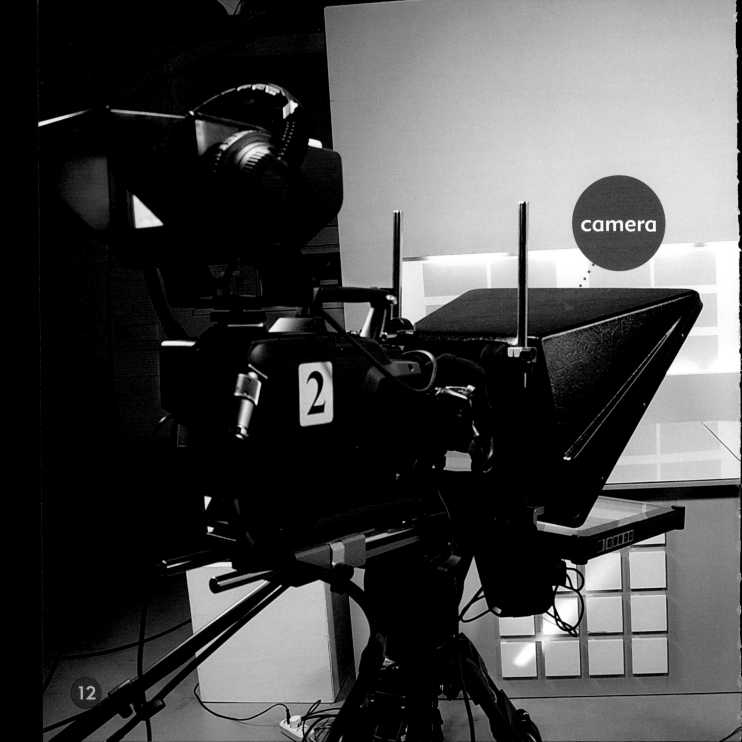

camera

12

Sandy is in a studio.

See the camera?

We see her on TV.

She tells us news about our town.

13

Clark works at
a newspaper.

He writes about
the White House.

Who lives there?
The President!

White
House

Look!

It's a soccer game.

Rob is a sports reporter.

He takes pictures of the game.

The radio is on.

What does the reporter say?

Traffic is light.

Mom will get to work on time.

traffic

Reporters do good work!

21

In the News Studio

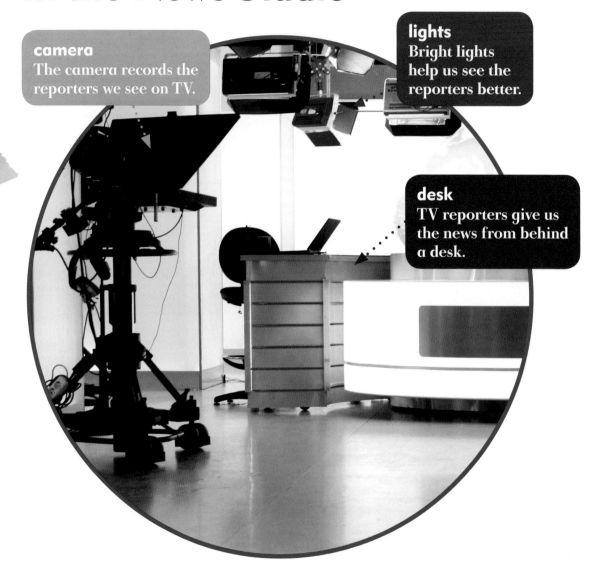

camera
The camera records the reporters we see on TV.

lights
Bright lights help us see the reporters better.

desk
TV reporters give us the news from behind a desk.

Picture Glossary

microphone
A device reporters use to record sound, such as people speaking.

traffic
The number of cars and trucks on a road or highway.

studio
A room where live television is recorded.

White House
The home of the President of the United States.

Index

To Learn More

Learning more is as easy as 1, 2, 3.

1) Go to www.factsurfer.com

2) Enter "reporters" into the search box.

3) Click the "Surf" button to see a list of websites.

With factsurfer.com, finding more information is just a click away.